Wisdom of the Body

Judith Roche

Books by Judith Roche

Ghosts

Myrrh/My Life as a Screamer

First Fish First People: Salmon Tales of the North Pacific Rim

Wisdom of the Body
Judith Roche

Black Heron Press
Post Office Box 95676
Seattle, Washington 98145
www.blackheronpress.com

Heartfelt thanks to City of Seattle Office of Arts & Cultural Affairs for their generous support to make this book possible.

Some of these poems have been published in the following publications: *Abandon Automobile, Caprice, Crab Creek Review, Detroit City Poetry, Exquisite Corpse, Face to Face* (anthology), *Pebble Lake Review, Raven Chronicles, The Jack Straw Writers Program Anthology, The Temple, Timpul Magazine* (in Romania, in translation), *Vox Populi Seattle Poetry* (Festival anthology), and on various websites. "Salmon Suite" was published in a poster by Seattle Arts Commission and installed in auditory form at the Hiram M. Chittendon Locks in Seattle and "Navigating the Light" was published in a broadside by Woodworks Press and, along with "Counting the Scars" was included in the libretto of *Navigating the Light*, a musical piece by Janice Gitech.

Cover art by Phillip Levine

ISBN 978-0-930773-81-6

Contents

the beauty of the clavicle

history is written on the body
each tear torn
from its socket of bone and soft tissue
salt water erodes what it touches
yet it is the fluid of life
the sea within
J.R.

The shapes a bright container can contain!
Theodore Roethke

Drowning in Lake Michigan

My first memory looks up to sunlight through water.
I'm on my back at the bottom and have already stopped
struggling for air. The sun's full hands overflow
light leaking through the flawless blue,
quiet and calm like a silent song, Mermaid, I,
I'm already at peace with my death before my father
plucks and pumps me out, sputtering
and crying as the water goes out
and great gobs of thick air sear my lungs open again.
I don't remember the coy ripple the lake lapped
at my baby toes before the wave slapped me down
and into her coarse-grained bed,
cleanly wheaten and speckled shallow
this close to where she cozies up to shore,
but deep enough for the baby my father forgot
in a sociable moment, chatting up a new acquaintance.
Always a talker, my father could make new friends anywhere
while I was learning to love the depths. You'd think
It would scare a child, but ever since
I've leapt to water as my element, looked behind me
to catch a glimpse of the ghost of my forlorn and missing
fish tail, forgotten in the rush of the rescue.

The Angels

are not like the Saints.

They do not discriminate
but come to everyone.

Their eyes burn green fire
but their kisses are icy.

They can play rough when we get caught
in the heavy crosswinds that swirl about their wings.

They are not above artifice
and sometimes appear in disguise—

a mask of smeared lipstick, gypsy
bangles, or an old man's coat.

Now and again they carelessly give us gifts—
an unexpected hobbyhorse, a day's free baby-sitting,

a poke in the eye with a stick,
or sudden slant of light on water.

And we are grateful, once we figure out how
to move within their state of complex blessings.

They work within great wheels and circles,
turning light to dark and back again.

They do not obey the laws of gravity
but laugh a lot and arise at will

to hover like vast hummingbirds
when we require attention.

What they want of us is the mysterious secret
we unravel and reweave

down to dark and back again.

Throw Aways

For the boys at Green Hill Correctional Center

Prisons are built with stones of Law.

William Blake, *The Marriage of Heaven and Hell*

They are only boys, though murderers and rapists.
Bad skin is an issue. Candy bars a treat.
Some are fathers. Few have fathers.

Ink pens are contraband,
though new tattoos bloom daily on arms
enflamed by needles and pain.

Beast and throw-away child,
no one knows where they get the needles.
Hate: Love   Live: Die

They remember beatings and fishing trips,
will hurt themselves if no one will do it for them.
Or one another. Innocence assumes forgiveness.

They are both the beast who lives
at the heart of the Labyrinth
and feeds upon the flesh of others

and the children thrown to the beast
to twist and turn in serpentine path
until they meet the hunger that will tear them apart.

One boy stares silent with wounded eyes, tied tongue,
and writes a poem of ten women whose red dresses spread
about their twenty severed hands in pooled blood.

Even the other boys say he is sick. They haven't
read his countryman, Lorca, who writes of sliced-off breasts,
the stain of three hundred crushed crimson roses.

Neither has this heavily medicated boy,
whose imagination flies, an unencumbered bird,
beyond betrayal and forgiveness, beyond his drugged fog.

He's found a vein, an underground river
he can ride to the lyrical heart of his own brutal poem.
The difference is his violence does not stay on the page.

Trisomy 21: Counting the Chromosomes

for Robin

What to say about it
that can be said.

It is like every other,
yet, like each, like no other.

They're all different
we say to each other,

though, we know difference
as a matter of degree,

not kind, and when it's kind
we talk of rolls of the dice,

luck, and celestial pattern
reflected in biological code,

which has to mean something
after all, because everything does.

Absurd as it all seems
at root, we laugh and consider

ourselves lucky to be so intimate
with the cosmic joke, singled out

for special consideration,
and given so much to ponder.

What love might learn
from the commonplace equation,

the internal rhythm in the dance
when the dancer does not hear our music.

And we know we are blessed
but, for fairness, not more than most,

because all are amazing
in their own ways,

though as time goes on,
the even ones begin to seem

so like every other, when he
is singular and unexpected.

Once I said all I ask
of life is that it surprise me

and I'll supply the passion
to meet it halfway.

How I wake in the night
when he catches his breath,

though I never remember it
and wonder how I know.

Mathematics is all, and asymmetry
here is the depth of difference
in the palm of the hand.

There are things we can count
in the outer garments of digits,

and some know the inner gesture
from before they are born.

In This Dream the Rain
for Robin

slants silver
but doesn't drench us.
We get in the aluminum canoe
and push off, glide out silent
in heavy scent of fish guts and metal,
you in front, paddling strongly,
and my inner ear hears your muscles sing
with the effort. My paddle acts a rudder,
correcting our tendency to circle.
We're perfectly at home on a boat
surrounded by flat water, rain falling like stars,
our fleece jackets catching them like fireflies,
lake, canoe, alive with phosphorescence.
She is Fish Girl. She would have been
Mermaid, but that's the way you say
it, with your hands. The wavy sign for *fish:*
girl sign, a bonnet string on the cheek.
Another time you named me *witch*,
hooked beak, and the two-fingered
bird sign. I loved being *Witchbird* but later
wondered if you meant to name me *eagle*,
so similar in the hands. We were running in the wind
that day, and you named yourself *horse*. Fish Girl
circles the middle of the lake but the dream
ends, as it often does, with you talking to me
in audible words. Why didn't you let me know
you could do that? I ask. *I didn't want to,*
you voice, *I just didn't want to.*

Silenced Daughter

There he was, in the shadow
of the doorway again.
Some things he said and some

things he didn't say.
In the daytime I
never tell.

But the dog knows
what is kept quiet,
and has run away again,

in a real house,
with people cut out
like paper dolls.

In the night he slides
through the shadow
and I lie perfectly still.

That is the way of it:
in the day he brings me books,
but the words tick in the clock

and stick in my eye,
die in the throat,
gone sad again.

Tie something to something else
and it becomes unraveled
from the center
and all falls apart,
like bone hitting stone.
This is the story of my life,

on this bed,
in this novel
in which I lie.

Jeanne d'Arc

hold me close to the holy.
I am driven forward into unknown land
traditional hymn

White doves came out of her mouth, but that was later. Before that
she bled in mud, as did those around her. Trumpets sounded and
men followed, and after that motets in cathedrals. Polyphonic.
Contrapuntal. Glory blazed her steel suit in the sun. Blue *fleur de lis*
and gold on a white field. Dazzled men littered the ground bleeding
around her. She flared so precisely, the actual flamestorm too blunt
to touch the clarified chambers. That is, her heart did not burn. Left
intact in ash and scooped up with debris of bone, letter to the long
distance holding the hieroglyphics of betrayal that hum along our
crossed wires and fly, ghost birds, into and out of the empty holes
of our mouths., trying to sing.

Marie Antoinette's Last Supper

I wanted to give them cake for a treat.
Now my jailers force it upon me.
It sticks in my throat.
Tomorrow they will cut off my head.

Now my jailers force it upon me,
making coarse jokes about foie gras.
Tomorrow they will cut off my head.
Once I played at being a simple goose girl.

Making coarse jokes about foie gras,
they tell me how the masses didn't have bread.
Once I played at being a simple goose girl,
Tonight they pull my hair and force my mouth open.

Now they tell me the masses didn't have bread
but no one told me when I was Queen.
They pull my hair and force my mouth open.
I tried to make a simple beauty in the midst of opulence.

No one told me when I was Queen,
how the babies and grandmas became bone.
My simple beauty in the midst of opulence
did not include real hunger.

It sticks in my throat
how the babies and grandmas became bone.
I wanted to give them cake for a treat.
I did not know about real hunger.

Mata Hari's Last Performance
October 15, 1917, Vincennes

When they came for me I was not ready.
No. It is impossible, a monstrous mistake!
I am no spy. But it is true
I always had a weakness for men in uniform,
men in possession of secrets or intrigue.
I have never been interested in unimportant men
          or small amounts of money.
Of course I took money from them
          but that is only natural.

No. I will know how to die without help
          because I am an artist.
Just yesterday I asked Sister Leonide to bring me
          a red dress and scarves,
          so I could dance again.
It is not true I tried to escape by taking
 my last supper as the sperm of twenty-seven young French guards.
That is a vicious, slandering lie,
perpetrated, no doubt,
by those who vilified me as a spy.
          I am innocent of their charges.
No, my last night I danced the ancient dance of the Magic Flower
          as I had so many times before,
          offering myself to love.

The stories told about my death are apocryphal,
          but I can tell you

I refused to be tied to the pole.
They knotted a rope loosely around my waist.
I refused a blindfold.

I have heard it is said I took off my clothes
because I believed Frenchmen could not shoot
a beautiful naked woman,
          but the truth is not so simple.

I know enough of men to understand
when they have killing on their minds ,
especially when they are in a group,
a beautiful woman will not distract them from their task.
          Most of them are herd animals.

No. I came to believe, at the last moment,
this death was to be my last performance –
          I meant to do it with grace.
I summoned the music of memory and began
          my sacred temple dance, as I had so many times.

They simply waited until I was naked.
Then they shot.

Sahara, Like the Desert

At the beginning of the season
where the daughter is kidnapped
     we get a new daughter.
The old moon
     holds the memory of her fullness
in her arms,
     chrysanthemums and asters
still flash from the earth and our baby
     is born dressed in blood
     and black hair.
I am there
but not, this time, the mother.
I am the mother of the daughter
     who has the daughter,
her long flame
     hair fanning out across the pillow.
I only feel the immense pain roaring
     through her body
like tightly scheduled
     freight trains by memory
     and connection,
though I cry with it in chorus
     to her pre-lingual birth song.

This time somebody hands me
the scissors and I cut the cord.
Somebody hands her
the baby to hold.

The Kiss

dear friend, thank you for dinner,
so sweet of you, oysters always
so sexy, our talk, light-footed,
arabesques everywhere, too much
white wine, our goodbye
kiss teetering on the lip
of abyss I would love to fall
into where I would float down,
my skirt ballooning out like a parachute
around my legs, buoyant,
so I would drift like particles in sunlight,
not fall. I love the acknowledgment
of that kiss, honesty and lack of artifice,
sweet and pure as your beautiful laugh,
which always sounds like some
thing bounded, breaking free,
a bird, perhaps, or a small child,
        the kiss
shifting the known world into another,
newer one where possibilities live
and we are allowed,
time screeching to a stop in its tracks
for once, and we would be new
but, alas, the resolution
back to this world,
bonded by tacit uncertain

necessity. I always like to leave
a poem with the world opening
in the last line but here
the word *open* is a struggle

Dear Robert,

Now when I talk to you I feel on edge of something cold
trembling on the lip of the sickness you sustain,
your body out of control and eating itself
and I want to say to you, it's not that I ignore
your wheel of suffering and unspeakable damage,
but that we are bigger than our bodies (easier to say
than to live when the house is falling down).
Whatever feeds the nest of fire inside we need
and what diminishes the flame we don't.
Pity equals failure, and finding the proper fuel, the task.
Everything is a test, for whomever
touches it. You, at the heart of this whirlwind,
but not alone in here, and we are tested, too,
head-on, and where is the art to give grace
in the face of what life does to us? I say
I am with you and I salute your spirit,
"courage and will" we said, holding
on by my fingernails to the beauty
of pure pluck.

Open Heart Surgery

for Orv, and John

They slit you open, cracked your ribcage
and whispered to your open heart.

Heal! they said, and that was fine,
but you stayed deep asleep

days after the surgery.
Nine days, to be precise.

But oh, the places you went with John
while we kept vigil in your hospital room!

Montreal, or possibly London that time.
Then we went to Marrakech.

In Stilton, England there was a cute young boy.
Very cute, but he thought I smelled too musty.

And I probably did, after all that time asleep.
But we had lovely cheese there, pungent, and sweet water.

Someone grabbed a water sample
but it, too, was musty, and didn't pass the test.

Then we went to Montmartre —
and what a thing! It's all

electronic now. Like in Charlie's chocolate
factory, cogs and wheels, machines purring,

and tubes, things whirring and spinning in and out of the body.
You know, John, I died before I awoke.

We rode down in an elevator,
Were there nightclubs and cafes and cancan girls?

Oh yes, but you must understand I was traveling
in a great deal of pain and from my hospital bed.

But I couldn't find John.
He was into the cognac.

And why not,
when you are in Paris?

But what frightened me most was
John was there but wouldn't talk to me.

Then we went to the South.
The South of France?

No, no, the American South-
Mississippi, actually, and there were two black dogs

who disappeared. John, do you remember them?
In a redneck tavern someone hit me really hard in the chest.

Then there was a ceremony at Swedish Hospital
for those who died, remember, John?

It was eight or ten years ago and then, only this Sunday.
We sat in the auditorium and the Nordstroms were there.

It was to commemorate those who died.
I understand they couldn't get out

because their hands were tied and they needed water.
A boat took us there, but my hands were tied, too.

It was given by a society whose purpose was to learn
the deep essence of the world reflected in water.

There were people with no faces
whose job it was to get to the heart of the matter.

I learned the beauty of water and it was exquisite.
You know, John, I've already died?

West Point

in memory of John Lesnick, Vanessa Peters Hayden, Tom Koenig and
Lee McKeithen at Discovery Park

what we can't know in this place
     where light unlearns itself in layers
     nightly eaten by horizon
     where a water-sculpted hollowed stone
     carries the remains of rain

what we can't know in this place
     where waters gather and go
     again, sent in swift currents out to sea
     and the curve of line and shore balances a half
     submerged log carefully placed
     to remind of what might have been

what we can't know
     concerns the destinies of men and women
     how and when they live and die
     and what light remains
     when their sun is set

Breasts Are Dynamic

says the radiologist

Sweet temples of adoration,
baskets of milk,
internal urge
of constant change, variation.
Form
initiates expressive content.

As in music, say, or color in painting,
gesture, in dance.
We love
the world immoderately,
our joy
to give ourselves away

on whatever stage we occupy.
Sensitive
and dangerous as any beauty,
our art,
to suckle and sing ourselves an opera,
awaken dense pools of milky night.

O mother with murder in her eyes,
          gatekeeper of our sister's lives,
—you can stay and you must go—
casual count of benevolent malevolence.

Oh joy in the word benign!
                 Oh turn of the wheel most bright!
We have a *good* lump and can go on.

Wisdom of the Body

Because the gut is the center
it fills and empties, empties and fills.
The core of us receives all we take in
of the world – absorbs the gold,
discards the dross.
Whole colonies of cooperating communities,
within our deepest twists and turns,
kindly labor together for our benefit.
We mean *Will* when we say
someone has guts,
closely related to *courage*,
but *coeur*, heart,
cannot be other than true.

Once we get there,
though so many other agendas
can tangle the way.
The mouth knows the taste of its own tongue,
hungers for savor, makes meaning
of sound, trying to name truth.

Or not, depending on the mind.
The gut knows the difference
between shit and substance.
       Keeps us honest.

Credo

I believe in the cave paintings at Lascaux,
The beauty of the clavicle,
The journey of the salmon.
I believe in all the gods –
I just don't like some of them.
I believe *the war is always against the imagination*,
Is recurring, repetitive, and relentless.
I believe in fairies, elves, angels and bodhisattvas.
Santa Claus and the Tooth Fairy,
I believe Raven invented the Earth
And so did Coyote. In archeology
Lies the clue. The threshold is numinous
And the way in is the way out.
I believe in the alphabets, all of them
And the stories seeping from between their letters.
I believe in dance as prayer, that the heart
Beat invented rhythm and chant –
Or is it the other way around?
I believe in the wisdom of the body.
I believe that art saves lives
And love makes it worth living them.
And that could be the other way around, too.

Epithalamium

for Heidi and Mike

May you sleep the sleep of small mammals
  gathering warmth from each other,
    breathing each other's dreams.

May sunlight fall on your trails
  and the sweet scent of forest loam
    rise from under your feet.

May your joining make joy, your canoes
  seaworthy, your kayaks be light and agile.

May the long sinews stringing your muscles together
  hold strong for all your mountains,
    past cascades of rushing/gushing snow-melt.

May the apex open to mysteries
  through and in-between the twined
    stories of your lives.

bees that climb the slipper

BOTANY

Consider the Passion Flower:

Who'd ever think a plant   *would go to*
so much trouble

just to get fucked
by a Bee

Lew Welch

Solstice Garden

after Zukofsky

blown fluff, milkweed slit splits
        empty breath loft, wind born
touch-me-nots , impatiens scatter

move from spirit to word
        poppy's pod breaks opaque traces
delphinium, larkspur spins sky blue

osmosis firms the cell, roots
        water climbs the lines upright
holds the flow of remembering

inside opens to upright swelling
        outrageous sluttish petal-spread display
stamen and pistils, sex parts

little spiral hooks catch hold
        five wounds bleed purple light
passion roots itself on pain

sip sweetness at the core
        disappear inside the speckled fold
bees that climb the slipper

Gender

gender is the soul's pajamas
Exene Cervenka

It's a Presence we pass back
and forth like a cherished talisman,
jewel, bone or box,
slipped from hand to hand,
trading breaths
and changing colors
like undulation of the aurora.
Unbound, we are, and shook free.
See how we fall from the pins that held us?
See how we are in the mirror,
stepping back and forth over thresholds.
What we invent in the undressing
and trying on each other
becomes more than naked
and less than simple, until night
becomes light and morning settles
in well-worn clothes
we'll put on again,
brightly blanking
a penumbra of shadows
about our shoulders,
brief brightness blinding us
before we pass
back to the familiar.

Hunger

All life born of hot thrust and eager
clinch is born to die
while those who come from
cell division can live forever.
The soul's flesh ripens
and chafes, stretches and cramps,
caught in the body's confine.
Still, she may be amused
at her changing clothing, momentarily
enjoying its theater, snake skin
high heels, gritty bars with big red wine,
a dusty lake gliding alongside a lilac road.
The soul, always hungry, watches
the fleshy appetites and says
no, no that's not what I want.
But we, animal-ethereal alliances
that we are, break our hearts and health
trying to feed her what she cannot use
and does not want, her dark night
driving us to outrageous extremes,
while hunger, blind,
begging and nagging at us,
gnaws our flesh and leeches
our bones.

Death Comes to a Flyer

our death
belongs to Psyche
it is none
of the Spirit's
business

Diane diPrima

Someone will come at the end
and tell you a story so beautiful
you will rise out of yourself
and go into it.
It will be your own story, told true
for the first time, and you will shed
all that is heavy and fly, flyer man,
with no airplane, no wings, and only
the best of you will come along.

It will be like the light held
inside an angel's bones, resonant
voice of a big bell, summer
at the cottage with no shoes,
and what song was like
before language.
Your own story told true
on the other side of grief
and the pain that stopped you.
Your story beyond what you've done
like you've never known it before

in words we don't yet understand,

but you will, finally flying
into it, rushing with wind and heart
and wild sweetness to yourself.

The Flyer's Ghost

Your house dreams your ghost.
Each beam knows your hands –
each cedar board remembers
the planing of your palms,
kick of your boot or blow of your tool
as you hammered it into place.
 The floor feels tread of your feet,
weight, firm strong step,
and later, lurch of your gait,
crumpled legs, feel of cane,
then, later, walker.

The bed remembers length
of your body,
your flying dreams,
before the pain, wild dog gnawing
your bony nights,
long rosary of countless women
before the slow descent.
Your fragrant sex
mingling, finally, with smell of cancer,
and morphine loosening
sequence through memory.

Your wife counts your women at your funeral:
        that one and that one for sure, and probably that one.
When she thinks she has them all,
another one tells a tearful story of the time,

a flying trip with you, and how kind,
and the list revises.

She has not, technically,
been your wife for most of the years
it takes to raise a boy and girl.
Your son, manfully, takes the spade
and scatters the first shovel of dirt.

Inexplicably, an ancient biplane
out of nowhere, low-buzzes
the gathered huddle of mourners,
who snap their bowed heads
towards heaven and the engine's roaring.
Wind blots out prayer
before they hunch
further into their shoulders
and believe your ghost
is attending your own funeral.

You so loved a grand gesture,
we should have known you'd find a way.

She starts a successive series of dreams
where you heal slowly, making
love with her at every stage,
starting broken and slowly strengthening, for nights on end,
until you finally become whole and solid.

In this last dream your bodies
yearn into each other,

skin no barrier as you merge,
skin, blood, bone, brain, and soul,
at last all the way inside each other.
Spark and shred of bright spirit,
love permeates your beings, saturates
every cellular scrap of you with shining light
and all that was hurtful drops away.
You're well now, and she has dreamed you so,
slowly, piece by piece, and it has been a labor.

In this dream the children are young.
Their little faces shine with trust,
apples on a tree, luminous with earnest belief,
so like the solemn light in your face
in the picture when you were six.

You have become so well, now you leave
them again, to go back to your own
solo flying dream.

What We Learned from Old Boyfriends

One day you walk down a road
and the forest closes behind you.
When you look back you can't see
your hard-earned knowledge,
suitcase to the unfurling future.

Its fine-grained quality allows some
silt to sift away
as spilt powder in wind.
The rest turns liquid,
a rain so light
your parched appetite soaks it up.

It's deep in your body now
but you can't call it up to mind.
Possibly it freshens your cells
and informs your most desperate decisions.
Possibly you've pissed it away
like time, lost,
tangled with past- tense kisses,
distorted.

The boyfriends ,
like your mother–
both closed off in the deep wood behind,
and waiting for you at the end,

of what you can't say.
What is clear
is you are without what you wanted
to pick up along the way.

Summer

Time held me green and dying
though I sang in my chains like the sea.
Dylan Thomas, *Fern Hill*

Those wetly heavy summer nights of long twilight,
dishes over, the adults safely on the front step,
and one by one the kids would gather
to play kick-the-can or hide-and-go seek,
a single telephone pole on the corner,
our safe stop, home free.

We ran so fast we hardly knew we were free,
or what it was that later might light
our way down future corridors to each corner
along the way. We just took each step
as the next logical one in front of us to seek
the place where children chase and gather.

Shouting taunts and chants our voices gather
a high pitch of *free! free! free! free!*
we'd tackle each other and roll like puppies to seek
the most delirious moments just before streetlights
came on when we'd be stuck on our own front step,
leaving the liberated zone on the corner

deserted at the precise point twilight turned its corner
to indigo night, the sky a seamless gathered
hem to finish day. Grudgingly, we'd step
away from the prescribed space we were free

and into houses lit with thin blue light
of TV, stupid even then. We'd seek

what we needed with each other. Seek
our animal bodies tumbling and turning corners
into the unknown. In those days our own mysterious light
would shine with strong song and gather
all innocent cruelty and joy to our stories set free,
flowing a river of milky stars to step

into before we found the lock-step
of what overtook us. And still we'd seek
our ways in every outlawed action to be free.
I'd dream of horses wheeling and turning corners,
of tall green grass, crossroads gatherings
and rich black starry light.

Since then I've found each step to be a corner
and each seeking, a seed to gather
root, what freedom I could find in purple light.

For Love

Seattle, the Hiram M. Chittenden Locks, mid-September salmon run

I understand these silver-sided beauties
streaking iridescent rivulets
      running back to Montlake Cut
where boats
      mechanically raise and lower–
      east to the lake, or west out to sea.
Earth of birth in the body inherent
      intelligence of instinctual emotion,
the salmon are leaping.

Each, one long sleek muscle
      gathers to hurl whole
into impossible air,
fling up and curve around barriers
      counter-balance against the current
          for extra push,
leap delirious
to ride the force of rushing, gushing
      water thrust against her,
to arc over the concrete ladder,

      a poor substitute for falls and rapids—
      but it works, best as man can make it,
          now, after all
      he's done to it.

She's slipped through bloody claws,
the fat-assed sea lion taking advantage of opportunity
        like any good market capitalist.
Airy sparks swirl
        a frothy blood-foam,
she's slid through his murderous teeth
while he chomps down on the flesh
of a less agile sister, her eye

on the prize of re-membering
the sight and scent of home.
Swollen with eggs, she knows
just where she goes, carries them
        in the basket of her belly
        to the stream where she was born,

green translucent light
filtered through pooled water.
She will hurl herself wantonly
        up any obstacle.

And I, though my belly no longer holds eggs
and the dream of babies does not drive me,
        would still leap off—
            or up–
the right available cliff
        for love
and hope to live through it,
        though I'd take the risk.

Upstream she'll die,
mottled and spent,
        and so will I
but there's this exuberant leap to execute
while bees drink wine from fermented fallen fruit
and September's golden blue sun glistens the water
    surface like liquid light on wrinkled silk.

salmon suite

Thanks to the support of The Seattle Arts Commission and the help of the Army Corps of Engineers at the Hiram M. Chittenden Locks, Seattle.

The Ainu of Northern Japan call salmon "fish of the gods." Northwest Pacific Coast First People say," the holy fish." For the Irish, salmon is "the fish of Wisdom."

The salmon's genius is in making friends with fate.
Tom Jay

Steelhead

Deep waders have found a vein
        to the heart of cold,
                the resplendence of river,
the grandeur of muscle
        and elegant economy of spirit.

They leave lives unattended,
        wives in childbed
                husbands in beery bars,
to step into swift waters.

They're there for the fight.
Wild winter-run spawners, Steelhead
are trout on steroids, river's darlings,
        the prize at the end of every sea-slung

rainbow, not stay-at-homes
like their cousins, but hero
on the romance of the journey.
        Deep waders understand this

at pre-lingual level. There are
many kinds of love in life.

Railbird, Copper Demon, Queen of the Waters,
Parmacheene Belle, Grizzly King,

Silver Doctor, Wet Spider, Princess,
        spoon and spinner.

The Samish, Stillagamish, Cowlitz,
Chehalis, Hoh, Humptulips, Nisqually,
Quinault, Skagit, Skykomish,
        Toutle, Washougal.

Flyline and cast,
        weight and diameter,
silk to monofilament. If spirit
is the fusion of thought and feeling

connecting one being to another,
and *kairos* a moment when everything
can change. Of the many,
        this is one kind of love.

Smolt

Smolt travel backwards until they reach salt water.

Being young, I don't know
        where I go.
I face my lake
        and float
        backward into my future.
Trembling on the edge
        of what I can't yet see,
        green-shadowed,
I go with water's flow and trust strange
        rapture singing in my blood,
        ride the river like a knife's edge.
Breathe and float
        oxygen and insect,
        cut and rise,
I've seen where I've been
        so, rehearse my return
tracing it in latticed strands
        recorded in starry lace
        fabric of night.
Current pulls me down
        to spill over smolt slide,
plunge the plashy fall,
        slip the snap of gray bird's beak.

turn to face ocean opening flat and wide
        beyond   imagining   no horizon,
    taste first fingers of bitter brine,
    flick silver and learn salt.
Because my throat itches
    I swallow what awaits me.
Begin young, I've cut my heart
    on the dream
    of the high seas.

Sockeye   June to August (October)

Celestial Navigation

*Salmon biologists are investigating the possibility that
salmon find their way home by the stars.*

I remember, I remember
the hollowed nest in stream of stars
the size of my eyes, I remember
the swell of water, shape
of light, celestial order to mirror
the song of river, the constellations
glitter into place to make the map–
          Scorpio, Virgo, Libra, Canis Major–
Sirius, the brightest, Orion, my own
clean cold water over stones, the whir
of the earth spinning through starry sky,
drag of tidewaters lifting
the estuary, sweet taste of reeds
and rushes, edged sedge grass
in dance with wind and water flow,
in silver pool pulsing scent,
deep home loam, the river
where I was born.

The River Dance

Aflame with the crimson color of marriage, the salmon
Seek their lovers.
For the salmon, the act
Spinning out life
Is an act of death
For the salmon
Life lives in death.
The salmon bets its life on love.

"Salmon Coming Home in Search of Sacred Bliss"
Mieko Chikappu, *translated from the Ainu by* Jane
Corddry Langill *with* Rie Taki *and* Judith Roche

Choose the site for depth and current
        water flow and roll.
Turn, push and burrow gravel,
        deepen the redd.
Settle in to test the depth.
Busy while the males fight
        to get to me,
                the prize,
        my hope chest full of posterity.

I choose the reddest one-
        Aflame with the crimson color of marriage,
torn and tattered but flushing
        deep burgundy slash mark pattern.

I pass back and forth over him
     caressing his back and sides
          while the others drift away,
          all their fire fading to dull gray.

Crouching together we hover
     pulsing along the thin dark stripes,
     our lateral lines, sensing
          every quiver,
throbbing our ancient dance of love and risk.

Spinning out our lives
     we love each other to death.

Ghost Salmon

> *The salmon die*
> *Ahh, so tenderly.*

> *"Salmon Coming Home in Search of Sacred Bliss"*
> Mieko Chikappu, *translated from the Ainu by* Jane
> Corddry Langill *with* Rie Taki *and* Judith Roche

Everything draws down toward autumn
and the way light is broken in splintered color
        we are broken to feed the multitudes
            take, eat, this is my body
                this is my blood
eagle and osprey
        raven and bear,
            stonefly and gull
                tear my flesh.
My silt settles and salts the stream
        cedar and fern,
            algae and fungi,
                ameba and protozoa
                    suck a rich soup.
My body emptied of eggs,
        milky milt settled,
completing
        the circle,
            eelgrass and catkin,
              cougar and lynx,

creating life from the dead,
Food for the stream,
     I feed all comers.

At the Tlingit Education Conference, Juneau

The plane seems to barely squeak
between snow-patched mountains,
though it's Solstice, and light runs
in the veins humming through the body.

Ravens settle purple-black in silhouette,
startlingly bigger than crow cousins,
squawking and scolding throughout the town.
Survival is held in syllables

now sinking under the smooth surface
to a pool of unreachable memory.
Each word brings back a thread
to ripen the weave. Light changes

and shadows turn a different direction.
Each phoneme lost, a whole world gone under,
like a native plant pulled up by roots,
carrying a cosmos its own seeds.

No one could sleep in this light.
Midnight, and we leave the bar,
the day fading but still there,
exhausted, but awake to the smell

of ghost words hidden beneath
the surface of the land. We will
leave on tomorrow's plane but
the inner ear vibrates lost sound.

Annual Walk of the Earth Spirit Women

Cedarville, Michigan, September

"We learned the history of the earth last night," says one.
"Geological time from the Paleozoic to now."
Another tumbles over a fallen log, but the earth
is soft here, even for old bones, and we roll her back up again.
The limestone is pockmarked with dents
where small creatures have curled up to die,
then eroded away, as we will one day.
Though now, with the light streaming through
shinning birches and blackgreen pines,
reeds rounding at water's edge,
we are all alive as we'll ever be.

Boulders the size of a house form a narrow passage.
We glide through to a decidedly different place,
where even the light has changed.
Now we pass club moss, standing small and tall,
princess moss with tiny antlers branching out
along our path, bunchberry and airy balsam. Fringed
Gentian, the blue of September sky, Lawrence's deathpoem flower.
The undisturbed forest is a mixture of the quick and the dead:
tree corpses collapse into the outstretched arms of the living,
a geometry of tall shapes with an underlay of brave ferns,
some who grow only here of all the world. Gnarled cedars unfurl
from crevasses in huge rocks and curl upward—some twenty feet high—
like smoke made solid, with no visible means of support.
The sweet waters of Lake Huron murmur through rounded ripples,
You are here, you are here, you are here.

red shoes

What thou lovest well remains,
the rest is dross
What thou lov'st well shall not be reft from thee
What thou lov'st well is thy true heritage
Ezra Pound, *Canto LXXXI*

September Shoes

Why do things get so colorful
before they're about to die?
Joe Safdie, *September Song*

Red shoes run faster
with burnt sienna hair.
Red wine tastes richer, a dark grape dare
on the lip of crystal. Simple pleasures

rise to the level of their own complexity.
Red cars sleeker, seeking the color
of speed through vermilion temper
tantrums in the looped-back miles of memory.

Red leaves fall on a slate-colored pool,
hold the nests of salmon
clinging at shallow edges,
redds hold eggs with great round eyes,

open for clues of the return road.
Flames flickering in a fire dance
red party dresses with flashing skirts,
inevitable unexpected laughing

in the cold crater of a silver moon.
Red fox foraging in tall grass,

the small mouse silently rowing
her little boat through the long meadow.

Nipples bleed red streaks in the milk, garden rose
bleeding on dry ground, back to the wall,
                    thorns flashing like switchblades,

Red ponies with dragging saddles,
an acapella song in the dusty aftermath
of internal battles on the narrowing path.
The smoked honey smell of autumn,

leaves turn wetly fallen on fermenting fruit.
Where is the edge of orange or purple
and what does she suffer to bleach out or bruise that way,
in the dark matter stretching between stars?

Wind

Hope, *that charming madwoman*
      with her flaming hair
follows a backward boat
      reversed river gushing to headwaters
and falling beyond the memory of teacups
rattling the margins of the page.

The debris of broken clouds
litters the yard and refuses
  backseat proposals to sustain
      the stubborn self and body
      of light, burning blue
and calling to the coyotes of night

fallen from the inside
with shaved shadows spread,
following daylight
to its logical conclusion

across the corridor of memory
echoing salt spray spun by birds
a knitted sweater, deep textured
wings gathering on the rooftops
      in dialogue with songs of feathers
      in their teeth, thin pinions
      in the initiation of blown motion
to take the habit of nuns, fling and toss
      of blazing foliage writing itself

in bloody footprints following
the swelling song hovering
in the wind, winnowing the reeds
and sedges in search of fertile seed
the green stain of the wind.

In Midwinter

after the party

What can we do but aim for beauty?
       Flowers in cut-crystal, flame shimmering
threads surrounding defiant cleavage,
insolent insouciance,
       even if it comes from the Goodwill.

Our goodwill tosses our heads like stamping horses,
gathers friends
       for the great temporal gifts of food and wine.
Our goodwill cleans the house, furniture
       polishes the piano and chops firewood in preparation.

I understand medieval masked balls
       glittering with percussive drums and torchlight
behind locked doors
       to keep the spores
outside in the cold.

In such hard times—
       and they always are—
our brave brief flare
registers the weight of the soul
       just before it leaves the body.

Public Transportation

to get to you

I crossed
the street, tracked
the free zone, transferred
to another line so hard
I boomeranged on board,
clattering my change
and chattering
my teeth,
I shouted
your name, my
destination.

*

overheard

What I thought I heard
        I could have said
What I said I thought
        I heard instead,
        free-falling through
        exploding systems
of what got said.

*

real life question

What would you do
if your young daughter
wanted multiple piercings
on face and body parts?
Would you say, sweetheart,
let me help you.

*

on city streets

High heels, work boots
Doc Martins,
sneakers.
Brown calf, alligator,
mud encased
creepers.

*

light slip

I rise at five, my window wall
alive with light eating night
falling away in crumbles as day
tears dreams like cloth too thin to wear
outside without a slip to hide.

*

alone I am
alone will be
alone with others
a suitcase
to carry
along with me.

*

Let an empty jar
stand for what's left.
Let fragments of music
stand for the people
in the story. Know
the time is fragile
and easily broken
like chromosomes.
Let the stones
be not forgotten.

The St. Matthew Passion

after Bach, after Zukofsky

Good Friday, the mass sung
and rain for 98 days,
rain so full the saturated
ground can take no more.

Good Friday and rivers full
at flood, hundreds of thousands
walk the road from Kosovo to Montenegro
and the border now closed. In the newspaper,
a child with bloody feet.
          as blood stained the ground as the foot passed
But it was rivulets of the muddy branches and paths
feeding in the road out of the town to nowhere,
the water poisoned and the grandmas dying. A woman
carrying her dead mother in a wheelbarrow.

Passover. The angel of death passing over
and gathering up. *This one, that one, this one, that one.*
The rest may stay. For now.

          cold stone pillow thy head
          dry grass make up thy bed
          bitter meal of torn bread.

"*Go beg his corpse.*" But it was long left behind
by the side of the road while they walked on.
          (Rest thou gently, gently rest.)

Passion has its roots in suffering.

The paschal lamb
sacrificed, spitted through, sent to the fire and eaten,
for this God is never full.
Oh grief there throbs the racked and bleeding heart
And the ground can take no more.

Passiflora, five wounds bleed purple light.

The Vein

I miss the vein
and rub the lump that bumps up.
The limit of light in winter denies
becoming a burnt match to show the dingy hotel

and finds gloves tagged and thrown in a ditch.
The damned die, die like rheumy children
tossed legs over hands in sorrow
under the wakeful wind from nowhere.

All the while night welts another halting death
and so dances in sand. Testicles from the garden
hammer our grief in the hole of the earth
and fall under a faltering mantel.

Some of us were laughing back withheld names
and sideshows verged on dimmed night's shaft.
We yawn down a hand's vein, begging heroin,
straight show stretched from grace to grave.

What We Do to Live

When they ask you what you do for a living
Tell them what you do to live.
Mia Johnson

Are you now or have you ever been
a witch against them?

> Yes. I made my spells
> so daughters could escape.
> I refused to feed them my sister.
> I hid my son from their wars.

Are you now or have you ever
laughed in their exalted assemblies?

> Yes. I've pealed like crystal bells
> crunching under their feet,
> shattered glass sound staying in their ears
> like ghosts to haunt their airways.

Do you now or have you ever
danced their dance or sung their songs?

> Yes, but with a skipped beat
> to transform the rhythm,
> a great vowel shift along the consonants
> to embrace inherent contradictions.

Are you now or have you ever been
naked for them?

> Yes, but I wouldn't wear their hat
> with the company name on it,
> inhaled deeply
> and only did it for joy,

weeping openly
for the lost children in them.

We tie ourselves to great wheels
and turn toward the wind.
We shift what we carry from arms
to balance against a hip,
change to shoulder,
straining each muscle group
until it's bloodless before we shift again.
We slit the throat of sleep
and let our stories soak into sands.
We are forced to lick corruption like salt
from the palms of their open hands.
Starved,
we grow thin enough
to slip through cracks,
their locked file drawers,
walk down dusty roads,
bathe in the colors of light-refracted tears.
We grow taut and develop
tensile strength,
which we use like lines
to catch loaves and fish
We build bridges to break barriers,
open prisons to find song.
We put back removed park benches
to fill the sleepers with green
dreams of great trees.
We grow flowers,
cut them to braid

as the long hair of graves.

We practice stubborn refusal in the back seat
We dance together, each to each.

Root Chakra Sestina

We are the instruments we play upon
living in and through the body
on our way to the next stop,
the places we can get in and out,
so many windows we close and open
and all of it holy.

The root chakra the place where the holy
body connects to sacred ground upon
which we scatter our sacred shit and open
to the green earth, the body
of terra-firma in and out
where earth-strength rises in us without stop.

A train dreaming of no tracks and no stop
or stations, rattling over field and holy
hills and flowers, escaped out
into trackless earth and flowing upon
unbound time deep in the body
where the world comes in open

and full and sometimes I don't have enough openings
and want to take it in without stop
all of the sun/shadowed earth in my body
and all of me turning inside out on the holy
earth, slick and exhilarating and dangerous upon
my mind/body gone trackless, my breath out

and in, in deep shudders in and out
and my throat singing vowels, open
song from deep earth, sky falling upon
us in showers of stars with no stop
and lying on the ground, the scent of holy
earth, rotting loam, transforming body

into something unnamed and beyond body,
a singing the earth can't live without—
green trees, grass clippings and wind-fallen plums hum holy
holy, holy, under earth's breath and the star's shutters open
like I do, and I never want to stop
until it's over and I lie upon

the earth, my body open,
taking in and out with no stop.
We are the holy we play upon.

The Baths of Caracalla

Anoint with oil. Crush the petals
of lavender and calendula to a paste.
Rasped grain of mortar and pestle.

Take notation on the vowels of the stones.
Pretend to obey the law of gravity
only until it breaks of its own weight.

Savor the satisfaction of displacement.
Light will break into spilled parts
and colors will leak out of cracked vessels.

This is the order:
> *tepidarium, caldarium, laconium*
> and finally, *frigidarium.*

You cannot come if you are accompanied by a crocodile,
have swallowed measured time.
Or have not learned the language of sparrows.

They will mold mud cups on your breasts,
casts over your genitals will change from slate to chalk.
Wild bees will sing fermenting fallen plums.

The chalice will fill itself with wine
The wine will ripen to, in turn,
drink the altarstone unbloody.

When you leave the bath in ruins
they will sing an aria in your absence
You will walk into the green world, clean. Whole.

Counting the Scars

The whisperings of stars
      hiss and murmur
    the histories of scars.

Erase my identity and rewrite
      parallel lines to balance
each side of the equation.

This equals that but no other
      can shelter the small sad door
in the boardinghouse of compromise.

Riding a blinded horse
      into a landscape of shadows
slits in the skin of the night.

What's stolen will never be found.
      What's left is an empty echo
an entanglement scratched in sound.

The river is lost from her bed
      and looking for love on the land.
The birds caught in her hair are all dead.

This is not a song that can be made of rain.
      I lay myself down in the small cracks where time gathers.
I have watched the night come and go again

Navigating the Light

Heaven is within us and all around us, even though
we seem to be living in hell.
Thomas Merton, *Bread in the Wilderness*

You learn to breathe through your wounds
and breath lets in light.
The light a river becoming
your little boat bobbing along
a path too bright to see
"God's eldest daughter" holding out her hand
to take you inside nebula, aurora,
corona, a sky radiating splendor
navigating the luminous waterway
while fires flicker in your wounds
breathing the light
and you are both source
and map to follow
your own fire to eat the wind,
        to plow the deep.

After

September 2001

Each blue and gold September day,
praise for my legs and eyes, ears,
reverse trumpets to receive bird song and syllable
straight spine, ladder I climb out of myself,

snatches of song and phoneme,
bridge to somewhere else.
Each rainy day of rivulets running
in leaf-clogged gutter down watershed I praise gravity,

sky-surrounded and in the center of a cloud,
and try to find the right name for the spaces
in-between the stations of the cross.
Indian summer sun and I rake my hands in the earth

warmed loam and claw my way down.
Where would I be without my roots?
How could I grow without the rain?
The gods are spinning away in their sky,

oblivious of fallen sparrow and obliterated tower alike.
Or not, as the case may be.
I even love the garden slugs
as I drop them in soapy water to die.

Leaves bathed in fall's fire sift down my shoulders
and a bee climbs a purple monkshood, all things

with their own names, speak in the voice they were given,
each separate strain braided into the fabric.

My children, isolate in their own sorrows,
the weight and freight of living, and I can't
give them the bitter coin they have to pay
for the price of their life.

The busy winds spread sad rumors from somewhere
and take them on to who-knows-where.
I thank the warmth of small mammals
and hands that can still open, this moment,
in the shortening days, toward the gathering dark.

Tail Pantoum

In my next life I want a tail,
a long expression of emotion and self,
to measure pleasure or curl and twitch,
before I use my substantial claws.

A long expression of emotion and self –
hunger hums at the heart –
before I use my substantial claws,
or long tongue to tell them what I want.

Hunger hums at the heart.
Precise geometries of muscle and bone,
my long tongue will tell them what I want
when I catch your scent on the wind.

Precise geometries of muscle and bone
walk a razor without falling off.
When I catch your scent on the wind,
dressed for action and switching that long sweep,

I'll walk that razor without falling off.
My vestigial parts remember themselves.
Dressed for action, and switching that long sweep,
rings of fur around my wrists,

to measure pleasure and curl or twitch.
My vestigial parts remember themselves.
In my next life I want a tail,
rings of fur around my wrist.

Judith Roche, poet, arts educator, editor, is the author of two previous poetry collections, *Myrrh/My Life as a Screamer* and *Ghosts*. She has been published widely in poetry journals and received an American Book Award for co-editing *First Fish First People: Salmon Tales of the North Pacific Rim*. She has conducted poetry workshops for adults and youth in schools and in prisons and is a fellow in the Black Earth Institute. She is 2007 Distinguished Northwest Writer at Seattle University.

11/07